THE INVISIBILITY EXHIBIT

THE INVISIBILITY EXHIBIT

Sachiko Murakami

TALONBOOKS

Talonbooks
P.O. Box 2076, Vancouver, British Columbia, Canada V6B 3S3
www.talonbooks.com

Typeset in Scala and printed and bound in Canada.
Printed on 10% post-consumer recycled acid-free paper.

Second Printing: 2009

The publisher gratefully acknowledges the financial support of the Canada Council for the Arts; the Government of Canada through the Book Publishing Industry Development Program; and the Province of British Columbia through the British Columbia Arts Council and the Book Publishing Tax Credit for our publishing activities.

LIBRARY AND ARCHIVES CANADA CATALOGUING IN PUBLICATION

Murakami, Sachiko, 1980-
    The invisibility exhibit / Sachiko Murakami.

Poems.
ISBN 978-0-88922-579-4

    1. Downtown-Eastside (Vancouver, B.C.)—Poetry. 2. Vancouver (B.C.)—Poetry. I. Title.

PS8626.U72I58 2008   C811'.6   C2008-901085-X

This book is for my mother, Monika Murakami, with fierce love.

ACKNOWLEDGEMENTS

I am indebted to the many friends who helped with the making and unmaking of these poems and who gave me so much support along the way. Special gratitude to Stephanie Bolster. Jane Affleck, Anita Anand, Elizabeth Bachinsky, Marian Churchland, Shawna Delgaty, Saskia, Joe, and Nick Ferrar, Jon Paul Fiorentino, Claire Gibson, Katia Grubisic, Kate Hall, Mikhail Iossel, Heather Jessup, Melora Koepke, Kootenay School of Writing, Jani Krulc, April Martin, David McGimpsey, Lisa McInnis, Sarah Partridge, a.rawlings, Gillian Savigny, Sam Sternberg, Laura Valdez, and David Wright, thank you for these pronouns and other ploys. Thanks to my gracious editor Karl Siegler and everyone at Talonbooks. Thank you Bruce Murakami. Big thank you to Sean O'Neill. Extra big fancy thank you to Kimiko Murakami, my sister b'zoo.

Several of these poems appeared, in different forms, in the *Antigonish Review*, *CV2*, *Event*, *The Fiddlehead*, *filling Station*, and *West Coast LINE*. Thanks to the editors of these fine journals.

MISSING

Waited in the rain with a sputtered candle,
set the percolator on the stove. Didn't drink.

Shriveled in the tepid bath. Turned
the stone over, crushed shells.

Avoided parties and small-talk. Avoided sidewalks.
Stopped washing *and* drying. Drove from ocean

to desert, didn't snap photos.
Tried jogging. Bought a stopwatch.

Threw stones at tree stumps.
Talked to the doctor,

lived in small-talk, opened gifts,
looked everywhere. Wasted time.

Sent a message in a bottle. Threw out
the dead fern, remodeled. Ate a peach.

Skipped stones alone. Picked up the paper.
Couldn't call. Thought of you living

in this midst that passes
so routinely for living.

Against Time

Her hour lasts as long as a wave.
A diagram cannot express this. Time is not a line
that undulates, can't be held. Even if the ocean reaches shore,
it isn't designed to rest there.

The record keeps time; its instruments keep us
bound to the hour and its decision.
Beneath the surface the crystal's vibrato hits
wheels that gyrate to its song, self-winding, and also
the wrist bone. We are caught automatic
in this top-notch system. Without a watch
we depend on strangers.

Losing one's watch is a gateway habit that leads
to social problems, her time shattered.
Watches pawned for pocket money, that cash traded
for a few minutes peace, enough time
to find another watch.

By chance the photograph caught
her moment. Lined up with the others,
it's her *before*, or *after*. She wouldn't hang
in the gallery otherwise. Now that exhibit is old news.

Deadlines here too. *Tick, tock*. I have to pull a wire,
though I'm not usually the heroic type. Knowing me
the choice will be exactly
random. Calculations prove
unreliable in a pinch. Bones seem silent.

I pass time in a circle of peers, tapping each head in turn.
Duck, duck. I pick the slowest one to be my goose. Is this cruel
or strategic? I stall, ruffle the teacher's hair.
There's no time-limit rule and I'm afraid
of the race proving calculations false.

Humiliating, that children could be so quick,
know the little tricks to reach the chair,
while I must cower at their perimeter.

Exhibit A (Boxes)

Leave the box beneath the tree. Leave parents to their cruelty.
For dinner, try pasta, try fury, try feeding after fray.
Try a split lip. Try Exhibit A.
Open the box: lump of coal, wormy dirt, slap of adult palm to knee,
you and your big disappointment.

After the box, another box, and soon you misplace
overcooked noodles, regular daily shames,
a voice raised to speak, *spare any change*,
the blotch of ink, splayed, her face,
you and your big disappointment.

When there's nothing left to open,
Open, *open*, when thought you knew the shape
of a word or what speaking meant.
You and your big disappointment.

WISHING WELL

My fist holds as many coins
as I can carry. All are stamped with the Queen's effigy;
Elizabeth, D.G. Regina, the resident of pockets,
a woman I've never met though I always know
her whereabouts. Each face pressed
into another person's palm before mine.
The stink of sweat and metal. The waste of it.

I wish for a return, or for justice.
It's safe to do that here. You can throw wishes away
and no one will fish them out
before the park's authority comes to drain the pool
and return the coins to currency.
Maybe I'm buying the future a Coke,
a popsicle, a bag of potato chips, a fix.

Maybe I'm trying to bribe God.
I'm not the type who says no to a panhandler,
or yes.

I scatter my spare change
all at once. Each completes its parabolic reach,
falls dead weight. I wish until the ripples still enough
to show my face: and just beyond, lit stars
bright as found dimes.

At the Moment of Wishing

The difference between genie and seeker
is a matter of solidity. I hold the lamp,
knowing what to wish for, but I forget
to save a wish to wish away its impossibility.

The fantasy began the day Mother
switched on the vacuum to forget her hunger,
drowned out the endless drip of wishes from our mouths.
If psychokinesis were possible, we'd all be
bending spoons on TV.

Locked in the lamp I know I exist, I hear
your hesitation: after all, monies must be accounted for.
(The ten dollars in my pocket I would rid myself of
wasn't mine to begin with.) The tin lamp glints,

glints. It's difficult to settle on
world peace. But the genie's grin
means good fortune for very few.
The lamp works better as a record of loss.

Two Women

You imagine her skin as fragile eggshell,
but the fact is more like marble. Like a bough breaking
in a lullaby, her trauma is to you theoretical.
Like fever dissolving into sweat, like a twisted ankle,
like the first sight of blood,
what can prepare you for this?

Open the door into an autumn
working your shoulders toward death.
Open the last of the Christmas presents.
The snowdrops too will open. Lie on the edge
of a rock, listen to the ocean close itself, and open.

On the walk home below cherry blossoms
fallen eggs crack beneath your feet—
sparrows brought to earth before
their time. Snap off a small branch, shake petals
onto the mess, let gather a pink heap.

The other birds chirp songs
your human ear cannot decipher.
Still, you crouch over the sidewalk
clutching a fistful of twigs. Soon the sky
will exhale its final breath and the street too
will empty of sound, with only you to break it.

FENCING LESSON

The rule we first are taught is not to raise
the blade until your partner masks himself,
but Maître's face is exposed, unconcerned.
My gloved and too-small hand is curled about
the grip: a toy-gun trigger. *Follow me,*
step back, step forward, cross the hall. The weight
hangs hard upon my wrist: I rest. *The weight
is in the guard, not the blade.* I sweat,
or weep in my mask's cage; in here, it's hard
to tell. *Again, one-two, stop hit; control!
Manipulate your tip and you will win,
or if you lose, at least you lose with grace.*
The lunges are nightmares he wakes me from,
corrects my pose; I feel my body's length
repair itself, from tip to counterweight
of my left hand. Sometimes the point will land
on target: *Like that. Good girl.* We both know
that I am here to win his praise. *Enough.*
The quick salute; at last I can relax.
*We're going to have a party this weekend
at my farm, in Coquitlam. Want to come?*
They grin and lean on blades, increase their flex,
They're laughing at a joke that they all get.
He leads me to the wire, and laughs at me
as I string up, test my tip on the floor.
I bend in the expected pose. We wait:
a judge we cannot see will fling us both
into the fray. *En guarde. Vous prêtes? Allez.*

ALLUSION

Two girls walk in different stories
towards two words
of satisfaction and the crowd

that would catch the bouquet.
The carriage rolls up to the corner.
In it, the prince's face, shadowed;
we see instead that shoe turned up
as evidence. What else? The parts
that fit into other parts, unearthed
self, her bartered sex. We knew

when her shoe dropped he had found her,
that at the castle they'd unfurl
the carpet's spilt scarlet to protect the Queen's feet.

And the mess of limbs and blood is only a rumour
that happens after. Do you remember that part? That girl? Do you?

Negotiating with the Ferryman

I shake the bag of coins. The dead whine. Our standoff
stalls their journey. Heroes scowl

or carry golden boughs as passports. I've a false
face that doesn't fool security. But these dimes

I would press to the roofs of mouths, if only
for the mouths and their findings. In the purse:

dust, newspaper clippings, cropped photographs.
Charon has a point. He cannot bring to rest

images of the dead; they never lived.
I concede and step onto the dock. The true dead

drift away. The boat empties, returns.
The river's ink blackens every shred of paper

I drop into it.

Instructions with Mirrors and Porridge

A mass requires meddling.
Upset molecules. A wooden spoon. A stone.

The others eat elsewhere. Look at the mess
called waking life. In dreams,

mindfulness, self steps into other,
break the mirror, scatter pebbles into

a meal of dust and water.
It tastes of dust and water.

Stir constantly to avoid devotion.
Until desire is consistent.

ACCOUNTING

At Carrall St. she eases into the seat beside me
her bulk of leather and scarves, heavy
with the scent of wet concrete. From her purse's folds
she pulls a pencil and notebook, begin to track

each lurch of metal and flesh, marks the time
against a schedule, tallies passengers, shopping bags,
redheads. There are names that she checks twice
against faces fading into cotton, soaked wool, linen.

She snaps her fingers, licks the eraser tip, but no.
They're all but lost. Her ledger will not balance. The bus turns:
the downtown skyline, visible, and then hidden.

Before we reach Mt. Pleasant and the greener
ascension she reaches her page's end,
packs up, steps down into the streets
and finds her place among them.

SKIPPING STONES

I fling flat stones into the surf, corral
my anger in the strangely angled pose.
Each beat's concentric blip a sound so odd
it clarifies the brine to mellow blues.
My mother's ex once skimmed his bottle caps
down at the lake; not littering, I thought,
the glinting disc's fourteen discrete hop-hops.
Now I trust black, the solid strength of rock.
My hand must learn the pebble's weight, and know
which chips will change the shape and spoil the trick;
this can't be accurately guessed, and though
some seem to work without my gauging it;
I fling them to new ocean bottom homes,
and some I leave to dry upon the beach. Skip stones.

Monster (Dead Duck)

The suburb I recognized like
the sound of my mother's footfalls
shifted. *Somewhere*, snickered the city planner.
Homes were ripped down to make room for fields.
In the fields, teenagers, overturned
bicycles. I walked quicker. They had plastic bags full
of legal explosives. For the one who was nearly adult
I carried my share of his shame.

The duck slept despite the bottle rocket
shoved inside, the laughter as they forced
it into flight. Then they sucked their thumbs.
I reached the carcass and thankfully
it was swaddled in a hand towel

printed with tulips. Spring left then.
I flipped up my collar, braced myself.

Portrait of Suburban Housewife as Missing Woman

Mouth open, she looked as though she was protesting
her inclusion. I brought her to a place
where no one speaks. *There's been a mistake,*
she said with the soft folds
of her tracksuit, the car keys
she held like a set of brass knuckles.
You can't take me anywhere I don't wish to go.
I did have to drive out of town to take this picture.
As evidence, it was the next day's news.
Now it's so obvious, her clavicle's hard line,
the shadow there, a hollow big enough for two thumbs.

Exhibit B (Bone)

From a quiet, picked-clean carcass
below an eagle's nest, all hid among the salal,
I pulled a vertebra from its uneasy line.
Rot clung to it.

Jam-jarred it in bleach and salt until lichen dropped off.
Dried, it was smooth and white as an unthought thing,
no evidence of the body that wrapped it.
White enough to force myself towards
the crack and splay of gutted flesh,
small routine battle, or worse, in February's last days
lying down once in the snow.

These are my stories. That death,
this history of bone. My pretty thing.

MEAT

At the butcher, the husband
has no hand in the knife
that hits its mark, that slips
flesh from bone.

He swears it has nothing to do with him.
Highway driving, talk radio.

Meal ticket. Retirement fund.

Other men's wives'
girlish flirty titters.
Ten dollars a pound.

Documents are fresh critics of at least six released promises.
Officials reach a deal, a hotline, a database.
Reliable statistic almost two months after the money, currently on hold, but

the delay was due to the need to develop related delays.
Another two months go by.
Waited round, requires review in October. The reviews are necessary.

Responsible for release, she's not moving.

The potential risk of the problem is real. The reaction is not.

The urgency deserved:
chastise liberal statistics:
five times more likely to die violent.

Who knows what common families deserve;
preliminary anecdotal evidence?

Suggest at least five hundred women respond.
Launch its sisters; a major dent.
Six women reported missing that we know of.
Every report and account. Measure Ottawa,
she stressed.

STROLL

the city marks his collar with a small burden of wet
he thinks unique without forming the word

weather splays thought   across earth, and a figure on the next corner   just the goal of
one more heaving breath's minute   just girl   not fit for   his purpose   (which
is this-or-that man

          give him typical flickering annoyance   at the weather   his place in it   and his
own   route through   give him the luxury of a name   and the privilege
that comes without telling it   a woman knows   her picture rests
in his wallet and if he walks   his course to her   and their easy habitual
evening   without incident   we give him things he does not deserve
          or ask for

                    or require

                    and we walk him to the right end)

News Development (Saturday, October 1, 2005)

You never know. So you just keep looking.

*

One disturbing niche—
other hunting. Lost for days or for decades.
Many cases grind, some break—
a handful of play. Mostly innocuous people gone wandering.

She maintained history. She had a cellphone.
People like her fall forward.
Cold plate. Cold time. Cold avenues, cold process.
Cold woods, a grisly collection of west.
The girl, a folded unit.

*

To find out who they are,
reconstruct structures, departments;
find the woman alive and well in Newfoundland,
find a baby with her boyfriend.

*

A missing person, the woman found—
Information / The girl in the woods
/ A database / Everyone in Canada.

The bank remains an impossibility of privacy.
Legislation soldiers on within limits.

I'm not giving up hope. We'll just keep going.

*

Cold present disappears, worked on, move on, retire or die.
In some cases, time is your friend.
Sometimes they stop being afraid
of modern techniques altering the game,
predicting the offender.

*

To release
trade secrets (extremely useful)

Modern database: Canada.
Virtually everything he does is logged.

*

At the moment a dancer went missing,
dozens of women from the farm refused the public.

On the face of it
a smear, a match, a sample.

*

I need to prove she's dead.
But I can't prove she's dead.

*

People need closure.
I'd like to do that before I retire.

News

Last week's headlines.

Wrapped fresh meat.

Blood soaked through.

Inked fingers twined

the roast he'll feed his family.

Twenty dollars. Sunday dinner.

It has nothing to do with him.

PORTRAIT OF THE FIRST STONE THROWER AS MISSING WOMAN

Remember, on the mask of her face, a flinty grin
you'd strike against if you carried
anything harder than a word? Aren't you thankful
for its disappearance?

The point wears itself down to a point.
My goodness, you say, and your loved ones say,
you all press consensus to your chests;
well, but didn't *she* have it coming.

WE HAVE A PROBLEM

We have a home and a home we hardly see. We have our daughters and our daughters' volleyball teams have the cup. We have the documents to prove it. We're out of tomato sauce, lunch meat and ginger, but our supermarket has those. We have eighteen years left on our mortgage. We have dessert after every meal; we *always* have ice cream—maple-swirl ice cream. We have our little vices. We've been a little down on our luck. We have a few pounds to lose, but who doesn't? We have to pick up the dry cleaning—don't forget! We have moments of weakness. We have all our favourite TV shows on DVD (we have a thing about commercials). We have a thing about McDonald's. We have a thing about litter. We have no one to answer to. We have the best because we're worth it.

Sorry to ruin this but you can't turn a girl into a gorilla; it's all down to mirrors and lighting. First she unveils the scalpel and parades while the music swings, shimmies in her silver bikini, Rockettes a bit. Now the first-row darlings start pulling out dollars. The crowd's aroused before the blown kisses, before she gets the outfit off and over with. It begins at her left hand, where she slashes round the wrist-bone, mocks like she's checking her watch, winks, inches the skin off from pinky to thumb, peels the palm off. Needs the other for working the blade up from the stiletto to the sacrum, follows the tribal tattoo's curve back down the hamstring. Man, the girl's got gams! The red lines get the guys, every time; she leans forward for a quick crotch-shot before she whips off the tanned chaps. Oh, it's *Jesse, Jesse* when she gets to the chest, carves stars out that she heel-kicks to some lucky fella. Only does the southern bits on weekends, when the cock-eyed kids come with their fat wallets. She's got the shitface grin down so they don't ever suspect. The neck's the finale, brings boys to their knees. It's the face they can't stand to see gone, can't stop pounding their beer bottles on the benches. When she's got the razor-wire coiled around her throat she tosses each end to a dude, and they lasso till the jugular pops, spurts the front row in the face. They suck it up, cry mercy when she yanks back the scalp. With her back to them she bows, steps into the glass box, and when the lights start to dim the gorilla busts through the glass screaming goddamn murder. Suddenly everyone's a sissy, scattered. No refunds, no come-agains but god what a laugh, what a bloody riot.

Monster (Godzilla)

No one loves a beast of a man in the body of a beast
who, at Hollywood parties, lurks in the kitchen, gulping punch,
spits sunflower seeds when a pretty girl forces him to speak,
leaves on a motorcycle. Looks silly hunched over it.

This is a fact, his life without love.

When Donne wrote *No man is an island*
Godzilla wasn't real yet, slept in the Pacific
until the bomb shook its little boy's fist
and he wandered into the studio.

We fear most that he might snap,
scoop up virgins and carry them off to Asia
where, unable to secure employment,
they'd be forced into arranged marriages.
After finding diaries with hearts looped
around the letter G, concerned parents
hand their daughters to psychiatrists, who diagnose
Godzillamania. They've pills for it.

This is a fact, the threat of him.

Downtown, night. Lightning strikes once or twice
to reveal his bestial face. He'd reflect
on his mission if the script said more than
SCENE 25. STORM. LIGHTNING STRIKES
ONCE OR TWICE. GODZILLA
MELTS GLASS TOWERS WITH
APOPLECTIC BREATH.

This is a fact, his imagined life.

And at his feet, a grocery list
rain-stuck to a bus shelter. In it,
virgins huddle and share a rosary.

Virgins are the first facts. Women are secondary.

He's suspect of the film's tricks,
forgets sometimes he's larger than life.
Can't tell when the film stops rolling
and accidentally squashes extras.
The studio uses the footage. Audiences gobble it up.
Shot out of scale, next to Godzilla
the victims seem as big as thimbles, and as useful.

Portrait of Hockey Player as Missing Woman

Done up in drag, he's half-grinning.
Really, he couldn't be expected
to take it seriously; it's all just good PR,
the suspension's aftermath.
His beard shaved for the occasion,
there's a pinprick of dried blood
on his bruised cheek where the punch landed
and the home team's fans cheered.
That's past. Now he's just a man
in a dress on the street,
passers-by on each side,
no Plexiglas. No one asking for autographs.

Riverview

She balances her weight on the booms
halfway from their point of departure
and the estuary where waters
take cargo elsewhere. These trees

refugees that escaped their intended
civilization. Dangerous pastime,
to reflect on ecology when a misstep
would send her under, draw a quiet curtain
over an emptied landscape.

In the clear-cut they've planted homes
that obscure her view of the aging asylum
and its gates she passed through once, cock-eyed, fierce,
to attend a Halloween party.
Her friends didn't know she'd been before

as a visitor. The guests wore plastic masks,
dancing in a hall where she broke a bottle.
Orderlies told stories of escapees
to spook them, but most of the committed
had long ago been released into the city

where a few became her friends or lovers.
She's since wandered home along the railway tracks.
Lives in a rented suite not far from here, where she comes
to rest on the river's litter as she did as a girl,
drinking with her friends. Still drinking. The still logs
slick with rot, still buoyant.

WATER, MOTHER

The mother moves in. The mother moves out.
Where her shed skin fell, dust gathers.
It's swept into a bin with other idle scraps.
There's no thirst, and no more water, ever.
Houseplants drop leaves,
no great disaster.

Light filters through lead glass
in the underwater house, in the lake's centre.
It's packed wall-to-wall with mothers.
Some glide by in stilettos with trays of hot muffins.
Others blow bubble-kisses to the sleepy ones.
The mothers wave and wave, half-swimming.
Their routine has a rhythm that slows to stasis.

Packed in the hold for sunless months,
I haven't a mother or a glass of unsalted water.

The petals wash out. The petals wash in,
colourless and dripping with sea-scent.
No one's watching. I came here
without my mother, beaching us both.
She's on some other shore.
The moon tugs the ocean, makes land seem larger
though it was there already. Mother, water,
there are some leaps I can't make alone.
I'd walk halfway if the sand stayed firm
but I'm no swimmer. Beneath our beaches
tectonic pressure is forming.
Even the shore is sure of nothing.

Same Old Same Old

The door is not a door,
it is a rotted plywood scrap,

and closed: inside, she hides
what she must before she pulls open

the door to her trailer to greet me,
and I am pulled through

into a kiss hello. I inhale
and assess her breath, gauge

the heat of her palms,
feel for sweat at the nape of her neck,

and kiss again hello. Conversation snags:
she holds up the cactus that is older than I am,

and blooming. The cactus that once sat
beneath our living room window,

the bearded patriarch of our houseplants,
is now so close to death, but blooming.

We roll cigarettes and smoke them
while she describes what became of the furniture: lost,

sold, stolen. We're sitting
on my childhood bed, wrapped in afghans

she made in the years when she was a housewife,
smoking the last of her tobacco.

Before the night is over we will drive
to the drugstore. I will buy her cigarettes,

she will ask for cash. I will drive home to the city
while she walks out with ten dollars in her pocket

and I will drive home with the dying cactus,
blooming in my lap.

Portrait of Mother as Missing Woman

Took this one then promised to send her a print. Didn't.
Haven't spoken since that day
in the hotel with a bagful of Okanagan peaches
I didn't want, wanted her to have. Now the leaves are falling
on the other side of the country
and her nights are some sad unknown story.
See? Once it's closer
the story waltzes in like an alcoholic
you love, hiccupping faux pas.
Can't not love her. Can't look at her.

EXHIBIT C (ROOTS IN THE HOSPITAL)

You lift your fork to eat small orange cubes
once pulled from wet earth, swollen with rain's memory,
a mineral resonance absent
in these blocks of sponge which to your mouth surrender,
defeated, jaundiced fluid.

If you could taste these carrots
you might understand my suspicions.

Some dead animal's overcooked muscle
dresses your gown's lapel,
evidence of a mouthful that missed its mark.
I fuss with spit and tissue
while you force dinner
to its natural conclusion.

The Jell-O is dry from hours of anticipation.
From four to eight, we come to watch you eat.
I scrape the cup clean with your plastic spoon,
blunt as a warden's tongue.

We agree the food here is a joke
we've heard before, with the sadness
of airplane food—
mass produced and never hot enough—
but on planes people know
they will soon eat somewhere new.

You Think it Safe to Talk about the Weather

So we chitchat around your joints
that ache when the clouds come.
The city can't dry out, and you can't
walk six blocks to the church
where they would feed you.

Yes, the atmosphere is an easy problem,
and the habit to complain about raindrops.
They don't stop.

We are given good nouns and verbs that do work for us:
help me. I can't spare any change for bus fare.
I can't say I love you

in a poem. They'll dismiss it. I have to show
I've dug deeper, to the distant heart
we do not call a heart
thrumming on its own,
a chamber that feels
like home. Rain falls there too.

Women go missing while we two
discuss the weather
to avoid the obvious old
love, that
troubled subject.

Poem to Stop the Recurring Dream

The house I've always lived in
has no inward limits. Doors I never noticed
have whole wings behind them.
I can't believe it. It's predictable.

The end of the dream is already written. An optimist
would say mythic. If everyone knows
what's here, then I'm not solely responsible. I never meant
to neglect these quarters. Always there are boxes. No one knows
what's worth archiving. Peach rot slicked pebbles ripped pictures can't stop

moving towards the end. The tenants are fucking
in the suite I'll never return to. Let the room be empty.

At the hall's end the room they tried to keep me out of,
where the woman's feet grow into the ground.
Dead for centuries, she can't blink and the hospital gown
hangs open. I could stick her
with a knife. She asks for a peach but they're all rotten

as her grey flesh & stink of useless mothballs   I move backwards into the room
where the pale woman falls, and every door leads back
to the room where she waits and I run dropping peaches
in a sticky trail around the corner to the room that would be emptied
where I hear as before
porcelain hit concrete and the tenants' muted laughter

DESIRE (DRYING OUT)

We know the sweetness
of molecular honey spread
on a synapse. It's neurological,
love. The stranger returns home
just to taste his lover's skin.
A single cell is all he needs to find
equilibrium. It's his now.

Sometimes we call it unearned.
True, it is painful to be in a body
not content to live in itself as it is, alone.
Confusion occurred; hunger equated with other hunger,
other equated with hunger. The volume
distorts the opera, gluts the room
with violent sound. Goodbye means
amputation, pain replacing fingers
where the whole life happened.

Goodbye, love. She stops at the doorway
it cannot cross, longs to go, begs the world to return.
He offers advice.
Lock up the house
and wait until wholeness happens.
Do not expect me to return.

This hurts. The inhabitant
only wants to play host. Come feed, she says,
pulling up treacle from her throat's well.

Only one emerges from the wet red chamber,
wiping his chin. The other
gone, not missed.

Knife Sense

Here is my mother peeling apples,
this is the fruit's ribboning circumference,
unclasped Möbius. The weight of the knife
means nothing to her. She could not tell

how she measures the distance
from apple flesh to thumb.
From the naked sphere she sculpts polyhedrons,
the skin's stain a pretty hint
of blood. But this is our afternoon snack;

the real meal is in the making. She acquaints me with the peeler,
a carrot, a potato. Her hands guide mine down
into the basin's depths, where the whittled skin
remains. On my own there are no disasters,

nor perfect rhythms. I bald them
with the inverse blade, then hand them over
to the woman with a knife as long as my forearm.

The knives that hang from a magnetic strip
above the kitchen sink are all just knives now,
sharply cognate, forbidden. Years later
and in my own kitchen, a nick evokes

first the usual curse; then the reflex
lick of iron blood tastes more familiar,
of the day I gained a sense
of metal, ballast in my palm.

Exhibit D (Peaches)

Now she is too thin from her smaller and smaller suppers.

Can't let her starve / can't have her over for dinner
or eat together something real—

In the Mission they pay for their evening meal with a prayer.
She takes what I can give her. A small enough distraction.

Her soup the full bowl I want most
when I'm furthest from it, in nights that have grown darker.

A bag of useless imaginary peaches.
A recipe copied from the *Joy of Cooking*.

Exhibit E (Heart)

It is best kept out of rational debates.
We've determined its place, since no one writes much verse

around tonsils or other uncertain tissue. We coo over
the sweeter meat that melts

into Hephaestic fire. Bless the pump that feeds the river.
It's not quite stationary but stuck. Can't fly on a whim to Hawaii.

In its suit, the king grimaces, justly
suicidal. The real world is not its place.

We say it lies at all centres, ubiquitous. The heart of it.
It's still only a shell. For all its efforts it can't contain the life

that flows through it, though it's fist-shaped. Keeps
trying. Beats out each Mississippi, is perpetually It.

The Exchange

Knit muscles hold my spine hostage,
all pain erased in the dumb knot that doesn't speak
unless prodded. It's pure luck I'm so blessed
with such small mercies, though I don't know if the will I have
is strong enough to bear any bigger wound.
I'd take your three-day migraines, the leg that snapped
in a corkscrew path, eczema, bruises
you got in a blackout, the exotic
hepatitis, along with all the conditions
you insist exist, but no doctor can find,
if I could live from there, as the crouching tenant
in your body, carrying the weight of each starving,
luminous cell, if it meant a place
we could start from. We could call it home.

Hamartia

Inciting Moment.

Woken by nightmare, a girl slips
through dark, past the closed doors
that lead to private rooms.

Though she knows
the house's contours by heart,
the kitchen seems farther.

Yet how big she is becoming.
Sometime soon she will outgrow this routine.

Enjoy her now:
the keen upward arc of her limbs
to the cupboard to find the smooth glass;

how she believes she is alone as she fumbles
with taps, finds the cool water
waiting in the faucet.

Rising Action.

Scatter her jacks on the pavement,
scrape the pieces into the hold of her left hand

while the other flicks the ball
high enough to collect the requisite silver.

Its weight is a guide she must learn,
find space in its pendulum swing. Dropping it

is a given, but she must not think of this
if she is to win this game of my invention.

I hold her hair back from her face
while the crowd watches, willing her to fail.

Quid Pro Quo.

Her father finds a diary
in a nightstand's recesses, the clever
envelope taped to the drawer's back, along
with two cigarettes, a condom,
twenty American dollars. He finds it because I put it there,

then broke the lamp with the porcelain base
in the shape of an elephant,

left lying around
odd socks, biology homework,
dirty glasses, a small silver key.

Watch him do what is expected:

lock the door, pocket the key,
lumber out to find her in the afternoon streets.

Intermission.

Outside the theatre in a field

bodies pressed into mud.

This is my story.

Things are getting heavy.

One emerged from the wet red chamber,

wiping his chin.

This is my story.

A record of loss.

A bone.

A bag of useless imaginary peaches.

This is my story.

A stone.

My pretty things—

Peripeteia.

Holds up each prop to the light:
the diary, a handful of jacks,
the glass of water.

Whose details are these?

Imperceptible lift of shoulders.

But this is not
what I meant at all—

Lock-in

Someone knocked, knocked, knocked.

Fireworks
on downtown's other side, from here
dull thuds. One half of one glass tower
frames a fractured dandelion.

Beyond, still cranes, a blur
beyond them, blue, grey, the city's
color code. Closer,
the streetlamp. Always orange. Six and six and six.

Where's he going? Nobody
answers. Echoes of pigeons trysting,
a voice repeating a motto.

SKID ROW

The name came from here, they say.
A road made from a black clatter of greased logs,

used for dragging timber down from Burrard Inlet
to the sawmill. *On the skids* meant *down and out,*

yet still not a no-go zone until Woodward's closed up
and the shoppers took dollars somewhere else
now called *downtown.* Now add an addendum,

Eastside. Elsewhere. The place where
a worker's toils sunk into timber and stayed.

SIDE

Our centre's healthier contract
Public-purse heroin cloisters
Outsided smokers

Alley stuccoed with dropped water
Emptied filters
Ensure drinkers

Eastern Starbuck border
Loaded port derrick
BBQ duck window

Rent drop shoulders up
North of Hastings
Rx for resting

Christian outreach stroll
Truth & candy handouts
Plentiful outspoken tellers

IT'S NONE OF MY BUSINESS

if someone says *Heroine*

if it looked less like sacrifice

if the alley were 30% cleaner

if in Cordova's commuting quicksilver

if south of Hastings

if she appeared in a poem or headline

if a fight broke out there

if laughter

Portrait of It as Missing Woman

And now what you've been looking for,
it leaning against the back door of the Victory café.
Stroking its cheek with a dirtier hand.
Head to-toe red and redder where scabs haven't healed,
or would be if the photo weren't so black & white.
Its body emptied of the expected contents,
purse spilled on the road before it.
It did this for money to feed itself.
Look at it. Like it's about to cry
or crack. Don't concern yourself.
It can't look up to find your gaze.

Exhibit F (Hook)

The bad captain's left hand and his name. Barb. Plastic Velcro half. Worm-impaler, tricky fish killer. Petty thief, angler. The catchy part of song. One who would catch you. Rugby player, he who throws the line out. Theologian, botanist, statistician, guitarist. Former name of Aerosmith. Cricketer. A punch aimed at the liver with knockout power. Coasting vessel. Beloved ship. Measure of whiskey. Where the phone rests. Folk wrestler. Melting glacier.

PORTRAIT OF SONNET AS MISSING WOMAN

Rebecca & Wendy & Yvonne &
Sherry & Lillian & Linda &
Sheryl & Laura & Elaine &
Mary & Nancy & Taressa &
Elsie & Ingrid & Catherine &
Elaine & Sherry & Gloria &
Teresa & Catherine & Kathleen &
Leigh & Angela Dorothy

& Stephanie & Jacqueline & Dawn
& Marie & Frances & Ruby
& Olivia & Cindy & Sharon
& Richard & Sheila & Julie
& Marcella & Michelle & Tania
& Tiffany & Sharon & Yvonne

Restrictions

seventy women with no concept of what a line break could

do not listen when he speaks and she shook and *shook* and she, through and through
it and ultimately a theory of

language will not kill you outright but this is art not survival we are well-heeled we
are posted we have no trouble invoking a royal tone or

puns and where our sex goes is into a theory of language as though we lived
there on the limits of expression drunk with skill with the boys

and yessing and or knowing and all these rights to language we have and enact
not knowing how easily we could choke

No Not Me

(i)

To see a world that destroys becomes a problem. Shock and awe, on every hour, becomes a problem. What we evade when the problem starts to speak

what most have lost, or don't bother to carry. To see beauty dropped; to see the problem of what we haven't. My dear, can you

create games to edge out real. Poke tense edges that surround and draw self out of context. Beyond, real consequence, the process you can't reverse or

weave through the slaughterhouse to the alter where he says some prayer lost on the beast. Where you see a shape flow from a rented neck. Or

tap a gavel. Look stern.

(i i)

Where were you

when the lost woman stapled her photo to a phone pole

              who put a pen down and snorted back the second-last bump

where you when what she wrote wasn't novel

              Can't clap your way through

Or get stuck

              Or dump the bag out fast enough

When she cut her thumb once more

              when she sucked the ouch out

              peach fuzz

then stabbed

              thanks for pronouns & other ploys

coax others away from what screams

move on alone

              or

yes she wanted   to be lost   to be found

Setting: Corner

—After Lincoln Clarkes' *Heroines* (Anvil Press: Vancouver, 2002)

A child's backpack stamped with a scrappy dog. Barred windows with heart-shaped details. T-Rex Opens December 18th. Goddamn the pusher. The photographer's flash. One menacing chalk-drawn eye. Art deco embellishments on the unused bank's façade. The window of the Ovaltine café. There will be no sandwiches. Park all day, three dollars. A policeman, a police car. A lock, a deadbolt. Her reflection. The international symbol for woman. A City of Vancouver pothole. Vacancy. This building is under 24 hour surveillance. Illegible Chinese characters. A mosaic that spells Empress. Enter to win, half-ripped. A Ford Focus. A chalked eye, an oversized hand. Open, buy and sell. The rain. Jesus in the alley. The pack of cigarettes he paid her with. Is it nothing to you. Ladies. Men. Another chainlink fence. A community gathering.

POWELL STREET

Now we are the audience to our own claims
of heritage in a park we only come to
on BC Day weekend to stand in line
for takoyaki make the bored children
watch the tea ceremony tap out code
with chopsticks on Styrofoam
beyond the chain link fence
a man sinks to the pavement
while middle-aged women bang drums
in the Buddhist church Shiatsu massage
is by donation on the lawn the picnickers are safe
from discarded needles everyone has bought
a raffle ticket for two tickets to Japan
Japantown doesn't exist except on this day
despite the outdated maps
everything we do everywhere go
is Canadian our volunteers ready
to attend to the first victims
of sunstroke

AFTER WOODWARD'S

The squat's since been dusted;
W flickers, privately funded.

We see you now. We buy your neighbour's houses,
hang your portraits in HSBC, deposit hope.

Public opinion turns on a pivot. Go nowhere.
Get out of here.

We clink glasses, say we care.
Hold you harmless.

We Were the Smallest Humans on Earth

—*Body Worlds 3*, Science World/The World of Science

1. If the living are brought to view the dead
   a)   and shadows trouble light
   b)   the display thrown out frame and focus

2. If the women are bent by strangers to protect that which marks them female

3. If child confronts an embryo

   a) If a lifetime / fortnight

   b) If without a heartbeat

   c) *If we were the smallest human beings on earth*

   Then if the self agreed

   Gullivered

   Then if strapped down

   i) skin splayed like wings

   ii) the weight of fat sawed through
   iii) marble dumped on marble
   iv) a tool to teach the thin living the dangers of
   consumption

Then if parts that name her/our life   become imagined
or snuck out on a cell phone

THANK YOU FOR VISITING. PLEASE USE THIS CARD FOR COMMENTS/QUESTIONS.

Can ____ be emptied of space and self and other?

74

The board members found it breathtaking to stand in the space they spent so long imagining. Gone were the litter and the boarded-up shops. Gone was the street itself, replaced by a new material that squeaked a little as they walked on it. The buildings were monoliths built to match downtown's wet glass: vodka tonic rather than warm-ale brick. And gone, they sighed, were the residents and their uncertain meanderings, save for the few that would be featured on display. *Yes,* they murmured as they were escorted down set paths from *ooh* to *ahh.* Soon suburban families would decant from the escalator of the line's new terminus at Main & Hastings. The ribbons waited to be cut, flapped on front doors like stupid happy faces.

The Invisibility Exhibit

Squats on False Creek where it once had labels pasted onto it: dandelion, daddy longlegs. Now the aging glass distorts the visitors' glances. Inside, the unseen anti-visibility engine purrs confidently. Its effects are drawn in lead at the turnstiles—that old superhero's trick. No magic until you've paid your ticket. Though the staff are always visible; consumers feel safer handing money to a flesh-and-blood body. You step through the revolving door then poof! Your body's suddenly gone, your hat sitting on the air above your collar. After the initial shock you just walk around being more or less invisible. Mirrors down the hallways prove it isn't a psychological trick. Psychologists patrol the hallways, alert to the first signs of panic. The cafeteria's always packed, full of laughter. The only food sold is stuff that looks amusing when eaten: spaghetti, curly fries, tomato soup, juice sucked through straws. What looks impossible, the body allows. Meat left off the menu since it is too confusing to hand an empty plate to an invisible person, and the invisible flesh, so like our own, is too great a reminder. One exhibit has a snaking line where they let people in one by one. Inside, they allow you to disrobe. You take off your clothes and enter a room lit with a bare bulb. There is a mirror. There is a chair. You can sit in the chair and look through the mirror. You can actually feel like you aren't even there.

THE ROOM WITHOUT LOVE: AN EDUCATIONAL EXHIBIT

Having foreseen the unpopularity of a room without love, they offer with it a 2-for-1 ticket to the Invisibility Exhibit. Few people make the connection. The organizers don't mind; they built it into the grant, and so it was created. Metal stairs lead underground into a room large enough for one. The walls are textured rubber, which, once touched, begin inflating inward until the body is encased, the head pops out of a hole in the box into an even smaller unlit box to breathe in. What is seen in there is entirely private. They'll describe instead the structure's pressure, an awareness of the body's surface and the hurt they didn't expect reminds them they had asked to enter, signed a waiver. Once they forget who they are and swear they will they will they will the box depressurizes and they're dropped into a puddle where they once stood. A voice asks them politely to leave. Each experience is recorded and available to purchase for $19.95. That's how they get the cash—they tell them it's the only copy, which everyone buys in order to destroy it. No one ever realizes how they looked exactly the same as the person before them.

Pose with Raven. Clap along to piped-in ceremonial songs about Raven. This place is chock-a-block with stories Raven wasn't supposed to tell. Raven coaxed the first men from the clamshell, and now Raven is manning the till. Raven Hour on the CBC. Let Raven entertain you! Then slip Raven a fiver after the show. Buy a stuffed Raven. Eat choco-Ravens. Raven-kebabs. Ravensicles. Black Raven Energy Drink. Let Raven pinch the wife's ass. When you sleep with her tonight, she will lie back with Raven in her belly and think of Raven.

The rental tent flaps its slips near the park's exit, half-hidden by the brightly-lit recycling bins. On rainy days people huddle in it waiting for the tour buses to take them back to their downtown hotels. It's low-budget, necessary, hastily designed. Some wander in expecting magic or technological tricks. But it's bare save for a glass case sitting in the centre. In it, some empty artifacts: Go-go boots, torn stockings, a red dress. Arms suggested by sterling silver cuffs. *Perhaps the prince kissed came and kissed her.* The other displays: newspaper clippings pasted to Bristol board, reproductions of *A Harlot's Progress* taped to one unsteady wall; to another, *Heroines.* The rest torn down by the city's usual rain, a few naughty vandals. The half-told story old enough to pause in front of while finishing the last of the mini-doughnuts. *My goodness, my goodness,* they press their consensus to their chests. Sometimes a few women linger, fall briefly in love with a fantasy. Those ones also love Chanel No. 5. The tent stinks of it. Their heels are high enough to keep them out of puddles, low enough to look respectable. They're used to flooring more solidly constructed. Someone takes a famous picture in there: four women on vacation who don't carry a whiff of shame on them, won't ever.

We've Seen Little of Her Life and Less of Her Death

The light plays tricks with toe-scuffed dirt,
forms a woman's profile. The wind lifts my chin;

resettled, she's gone, ruins already.

In a theatre an artist projects
an armless Venus onto a dancer's gown.

Somewhere, sifting through earth, a man finds
a false fingernail, is shocked by the enduring red.

Now the lab is nearly empty.
What gentleness we muster now, to lift DNA

from a microscopic edge, to protect
the whole of the woman contained there.